HAL•LEONARD

Book and CD for B♭, E♭, C and Bass Clef Instruments

volume
141

Arranged and Produced by
Mark Taylor and Jim Roberts

bill evans
STANDARDS

BOOK

CD

Cover photo © Jan Persson/CTSIMAGES

ISBN 978-1-4234-6867-7

HAL•LEONARD®
CORPORATION

7777 W. BLUEMOUND RD. P.O. BOX 13819 MILWAUKEE, WI 53213

Visit Hal Leonard Online at
www.halleonard.com

BILL EVANS STANDARDS

Volume 141

Arranged and Produced by
Mark Taylor and Jim Roberts

Featured Players:

Graham Breedlove–Trumpet and Flugelhorn
John Desalme–Tenor Sax
Tony Nalker–Piano
Jim Roberts–Bass
Todd Harrison–Drums

Recorded at Bias Studios, Springfield, Virginia
Bob Dawson, Engineer

HOW TO USE THE CD:
Each song has two tracks:

1) Split Track/Melody

Woodwind, Brass, Keyboard, and **Mallet Players** can use this track as a learning tool for melody style and inflection.

Bass Players can learn and perform with this track – remove the recorded bass track by turning down the volume on the LEFT channel.

Keyboard and **Guitar Players** can learn and perform with this track – remove the recorded piano part by turning down the volume on the RIGHT channel.

2) Full Stereo Track

Soloists or **Groups** can learn and perform with this accompaniment track with the RHYTHM SECTION only.

EMILY
FROM THE MGM MOTION PICTURE THE AMERICANIZATION OF EMILY

MUSIC BY JOHNNY MANDEL
WORDS BY JOHNNY MERCER

C VERSION

SOLOS (2 CHORUSES)

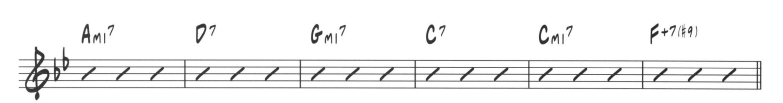

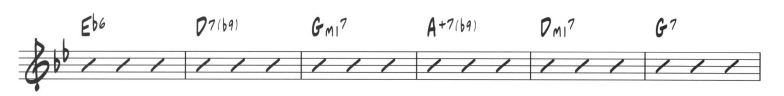

D.C. AL CODA

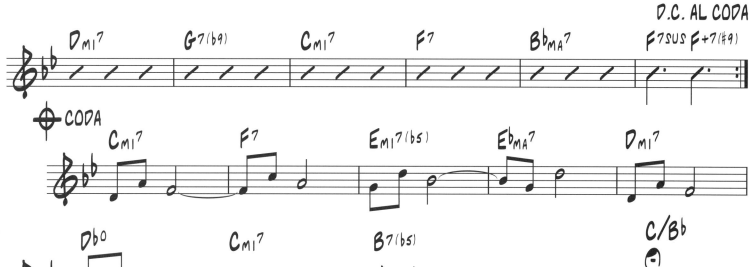

CODA

RIT.

IN LOVE IN VAIN

CD

◆3 : SPLIT TRACK/MELODY
◆4 : FULL STEREO TRACK

C VERSION

WORDS BY LEO ROBIN
MUSIC BY JEROME KERN

MEDIUM BALLAD

CD

5 : SPLIT TRACK/MELODY
6 : FULL STEREO TRACK

C VERSION

MY FOOLISH HEART
FROM MY FOOLISH HEART

WORDS BY NED WASHINGTON
MUSIC BY VICTOR YOUNG

MEDIUM BALLAD

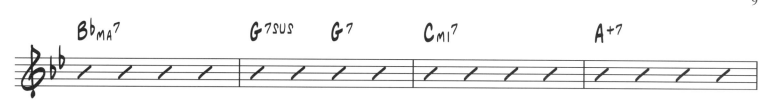

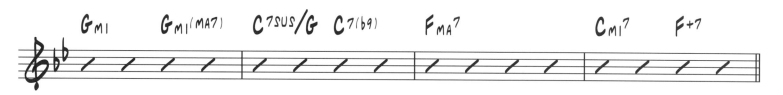

MY HEART STOOD STILL

FROM A CONNECTICUT YANKEE

WORDS BY LORENZ HART
MUSIC BY RICHARD RODGERS

CD
7 : SPLIT TRACK/MELODY
8 : FULL STEREO TRACK

C VERSION

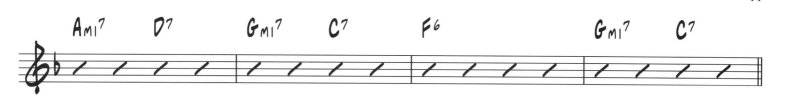

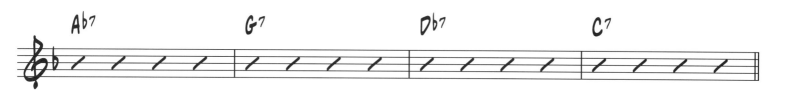

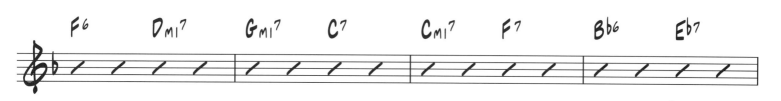

D.C. AL CODA
TAKE REPEAT

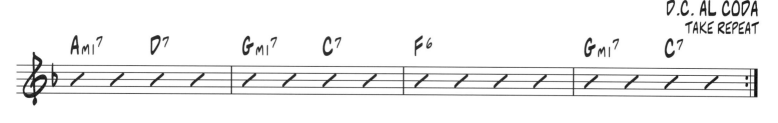

Sweet and Lovely

WORDS AND MUSIC BY GUS ARNHEIM,
CHARLES N. DANIELS AND HARRY TOBIAS

CD

C VERSION

Tenderly
FROM TORCH SONG

LYRIC BY JACK LAWRENCE
MUSIC BY WALTER GROSS

MEDIUM WALTZ TEMPO

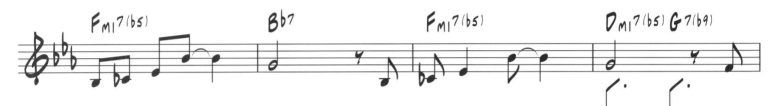

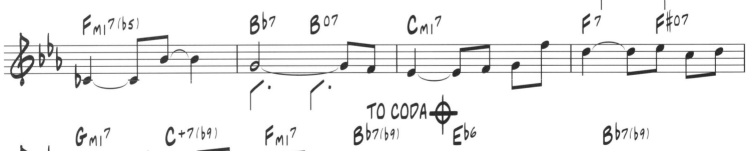

SOLOS (3 CHORUSES)

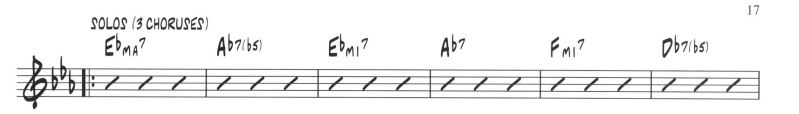

LAST X ONLY

CD
17 : SPLIT TRACK/MELODY
18 : FULL STEREO TRACK

C VERSION

WHO CAN I TURN TO
(WHEN NOBODY NEEDS ME)

FROM THE ROAR OF THE GREASEPAINT – THE SMELL OF THE CROWD

WORDS AND MUSIC BY LESLIE BRICUSSE
AND ANTHONY NEWLEY

MEDIUM SWING

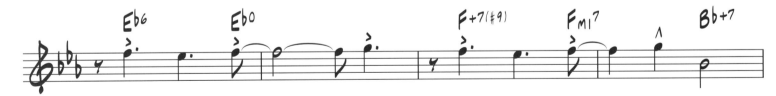

CD

19 : SPLIT TRACK/MELODY
20 : FULL STEREO TRACK

WITCHCRAFT

MUSIC BY CY COLEMAN
LYRICS BY CAROLYN LEIGH

C VERSION

MEDIUM SWING

TO CODA

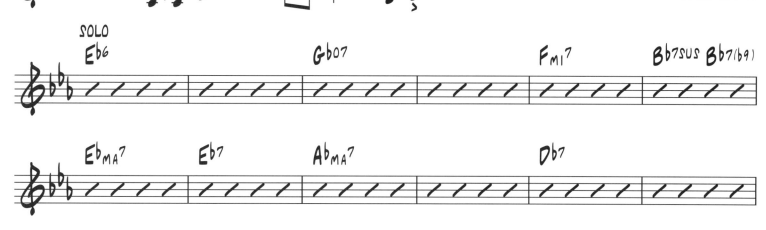

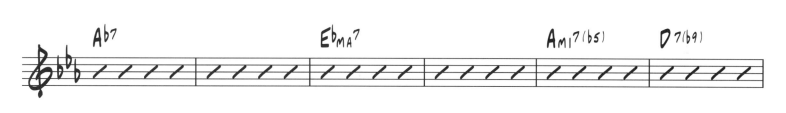

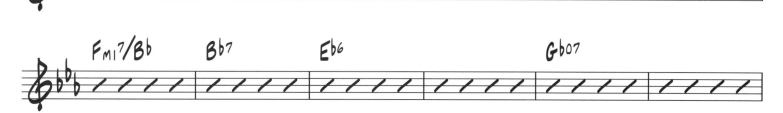

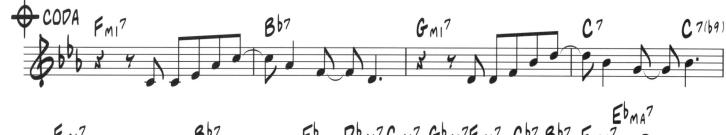

CD

11 : SPLIT TRACK/MELODY
12 : FULL STEREO TRACK

C VERSION

SUICIDE IS PAINLESS
(SONG FROM M*A*S*H)

WORDS AND MUSIC BY MIKE ALTMAN
AND JOHNNY MANDEL

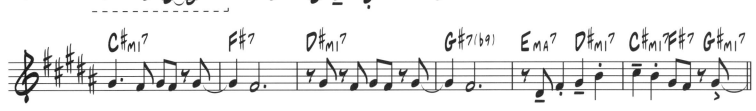

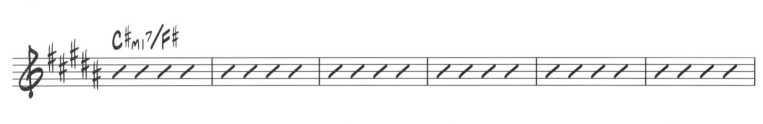

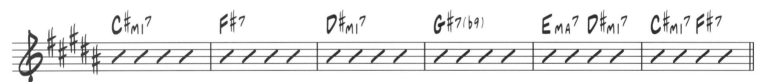

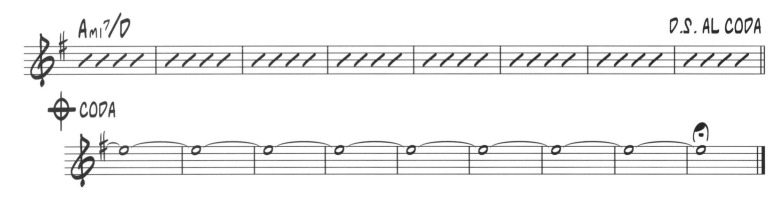

SUICIDE IS PAINLESS
(SONG FROM M*A*S*H)

WORDS AND MUSIC BY MIKE ALTMAN
AND JOHNNY MANDEL

Bb VERSION

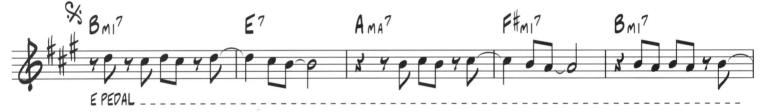

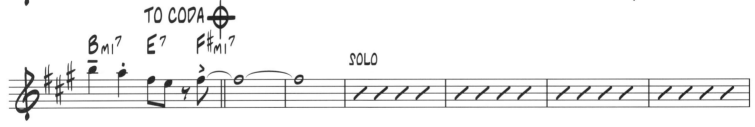

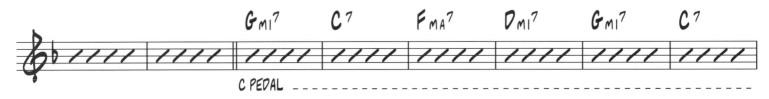

1 : SPLIT TRACK/MELODY
2 : FULL STEREO TRACK

Bb VERSION

EMILY
FROM THE MGM MOTION PICTURE THE AMERICANIZATION OF EMILY

MUSIC BY JOHNNY MANDEL
WORDS BY JOHNNY MERCER

MEDIUM JAZZ WALTZ

29

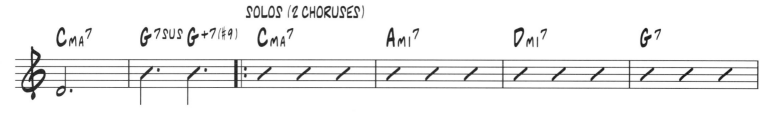

CD

◆3 : SPLIT TRACK/MELODY
◆4 : FULL STEREO TRACK

In Love in Vain

WORDS BY LEO ROBIN
MUSIC BY JEROME KERN

Bb VERSION

MEDIUM BALLAD

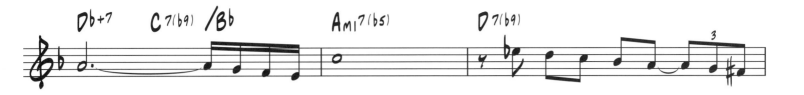

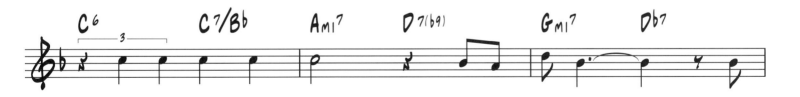

MY FOOLISH HEART

FROM MY FOOLISH HEART

WORDS BY NED WASHINGTON
MUSIC BY VICTOR YOUNG

Bb VERSION

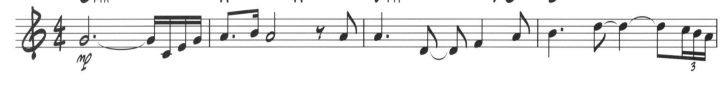

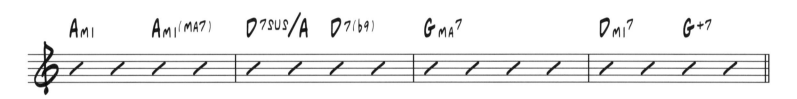

MY HEART STOOD STILL

FROM A CONNECTICUT YANKEE

WORDS BY LORENZ HART
MUSIC BY RICHARD RODGERS

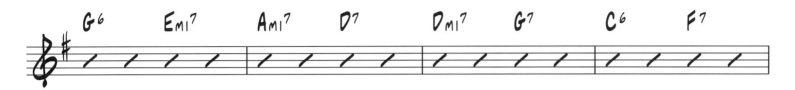

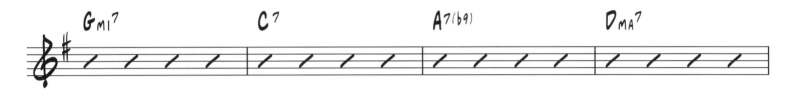

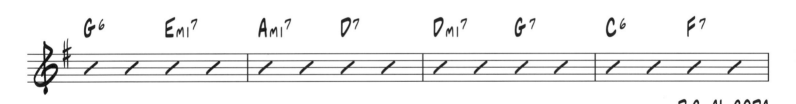

D.C. AL CODA
TAKE REPEAT

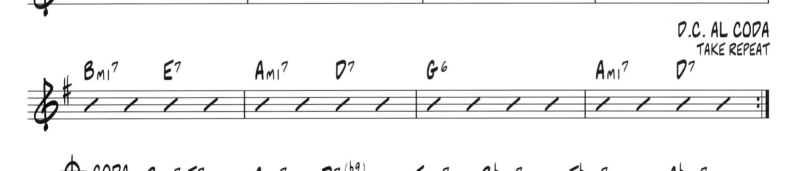

A SLEEPIN' BEE
FROM HOUSE OF FLOWERS

LYRIC BY TRUMAN CAPOTE AND HAROLD ARLEN
MUSIC BY HAROLD ARLEN

CD
13 : SPLIT TRACK/MELODY
14 : FULL STEREO TRACK

Sweet and Lovely

WORDS AND MUSIC BY GUS ARNHEIM,
CHARLES N. DANIELS AND HARRY TOBIAS

Bb VERSION

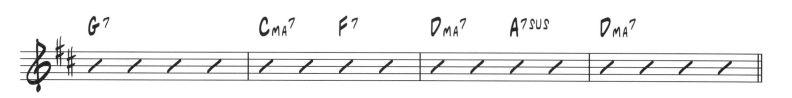

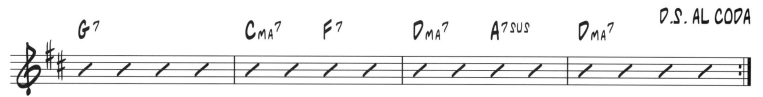

CD

15 : SPLIT TRACK/MELODY
16 : FULL STEREO TRACK

Bb VERSION

TENDERLY
FROM TORCH SONG

LYRIC BY JACK LAWRENCE
MUSIC BY WALTER GROSS

MEDIUM WALTZ TEMPO

41

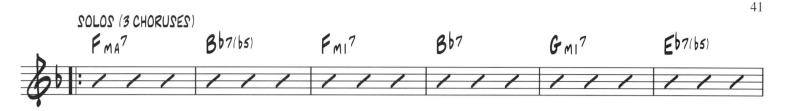

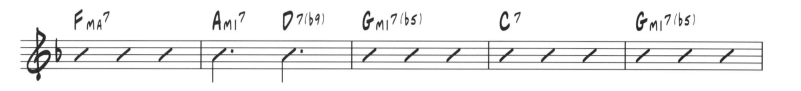

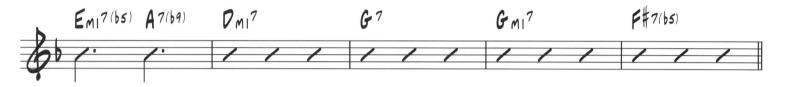

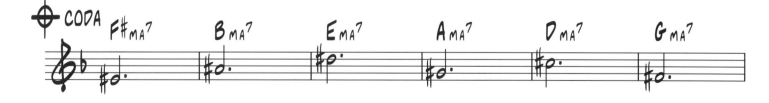

Who Can I Turn To
(When Nobody Needs Me)
FROM THE ROAR OF THE GREASEPAINT - THE SMELL OF THE CROWD

WORDS AND MUSIC BY LESLIE BRICUSSE
AND ANTHONY NEWLEY

Bb VERSION

CD

19 : SPLIT TRACK/MELODY
20 : FULL STEREO TRACK

WITCHCRAFT

MUSIC BY CY COLEMAN
LYRICS BY CAROLYN LEIGH

Bb VERSION

MEDIUM SWING

TO CODA ⊕

45

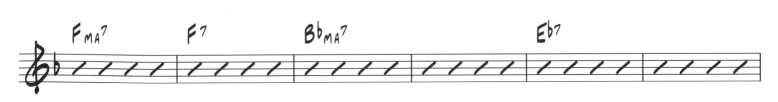

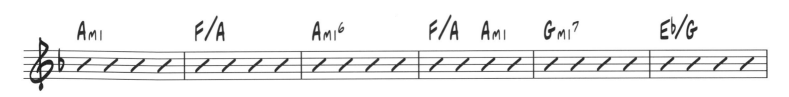

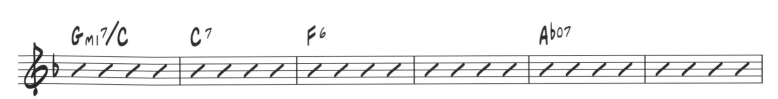

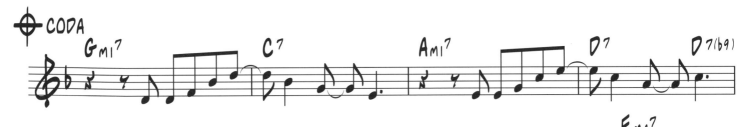

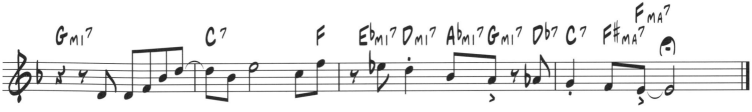

CD

1 : SPLIT TRACK/MELODY
2 : FULL STEREO TRACK

Eb VERSION

EMILY

FROM THE MGM MOTION PICTURE THE AMERICANIZATION OF EMILY

MUSIC BY JOHNNY MANDEL
WORDS BY JOHNNY MERCER

MEDIUM JAZZ WALTZ

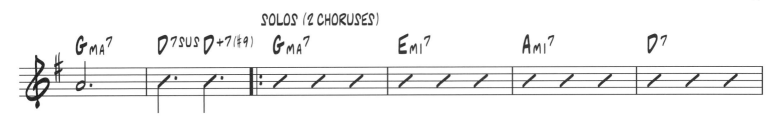

SOLOS (2 CHORUSES)

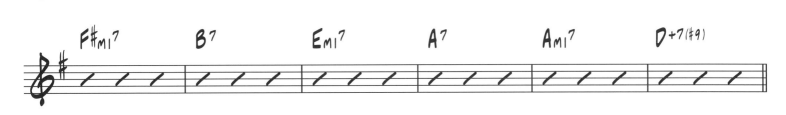

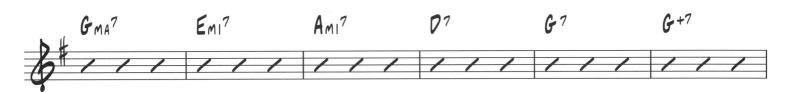

In Love In Vain

WORDS BY LEO ROBIN
MUSIC BY JEROME KERN

Eb VERSION

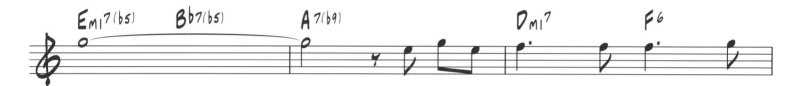

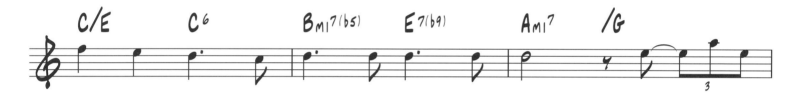

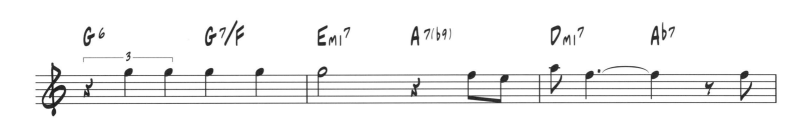

MY FOOLISH HEART

FROM MY FOOLISH HEART

WORDS BY NED WASHINGTON
MUSIC BY VICTOR YOUNG

Eb VERSION

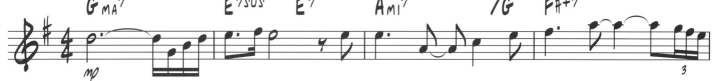

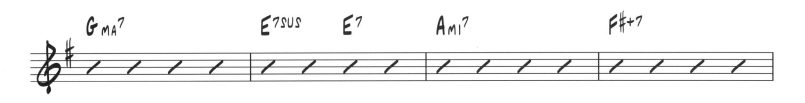

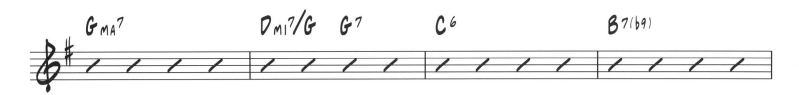

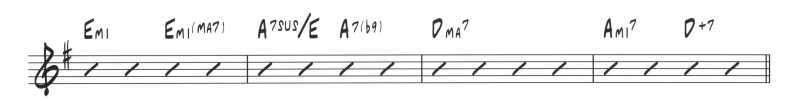

RIT.

MY HEART STOOD STILL

FROM A CONNECTICUT YANKEE

WORDS BY LORENZ HART
MUSIC BY RICHARD RODGERS

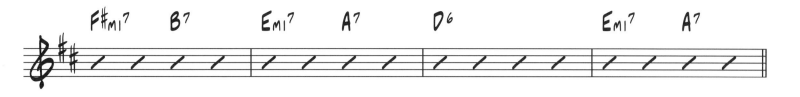

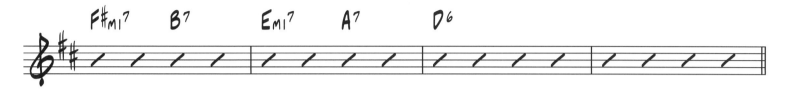

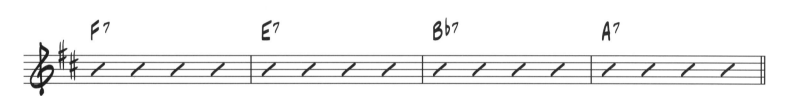

D.C. AL CODA
TAKE REPEAT

A SLEEPIN' BEE
FROM HOUSE OF FLOWERS

LYRIC BY TRUMAN CAPOTE AND HAROLD ARLEN
MUSIC BY HAROLD ARLEN

CD
- 9 : SPLIT TRACK/MELODY
- 10 : FULL STEREO TRACK

Eb VERSION

Sweet and Lovely

WORDS AND MUSIC BY GUS ARNHEIM,
CHARLES N. DANIELS AND HARRY TOBIAS

Eb VERSION

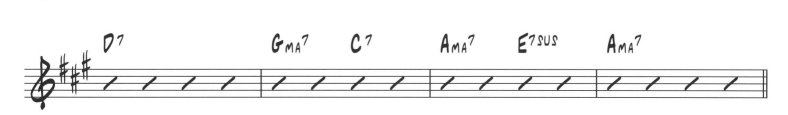

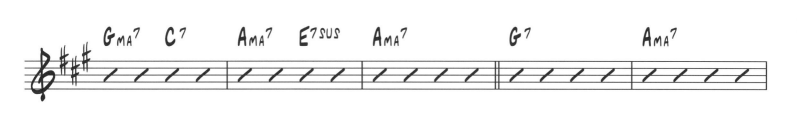

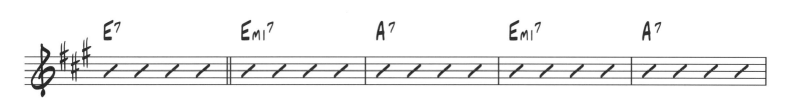

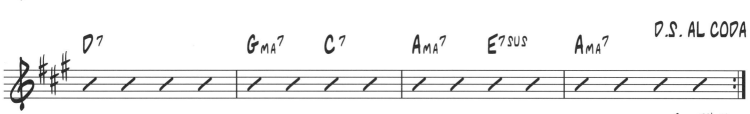

CD

Eb VERSION

Tenderly
FROM TORCH SONG

LYRIC BY JACK LAWRENCE
MUSIC BY WALTER GROSS

MEDIUM WALTZ TEMPO

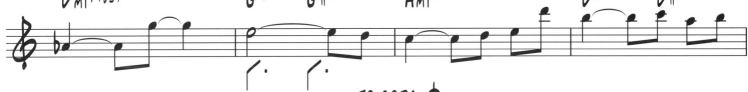

SOLOS (3 CHORUSES)

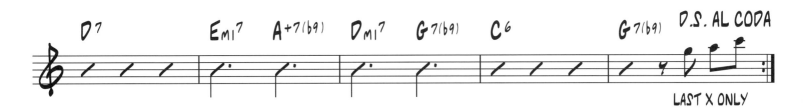

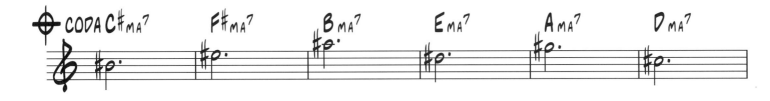

WHO CAN I TURN TO
(WHEN NOBODY NEEDS ME)

FROM THE ROAR OF THE GREASEPAINT – THE SMELL OF THE CROWD

WORDS AND MUSIC BY LESLIE BRICUSSE
AND ANTHONY NEWLEY

Eb VERSION

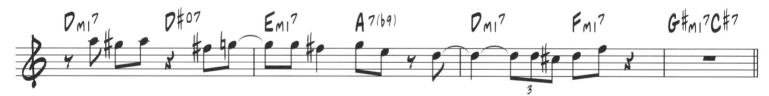

CD

WITCHCRAFT

MUSIC BY CY COLEMAN
LYRICS BY CAROLYN LEIGH

Eb VERSION

MEDIUM SWING

TO CODA ⊕

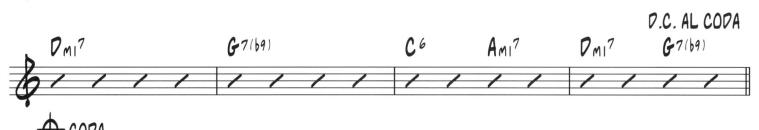

SUICIDE IS PAINLESS
(SONG FROM M*A*S*H)

WORDS AND MUSIC BY MIKE ALTMAN
AND JOHNNY MANDEL

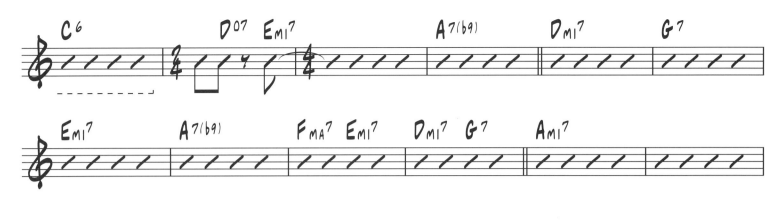

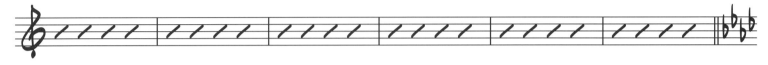

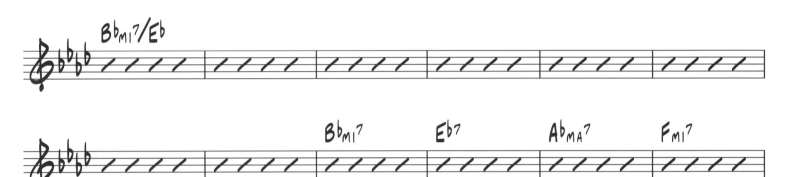

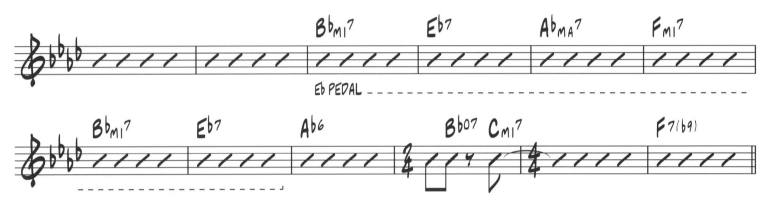

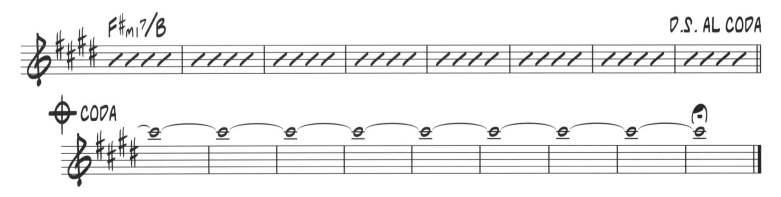

SUICIDE IS PAINLESS
(SONG FROM M*A*S*H)

WORDS AND MUSIC BY MIKE ALTMAN
AND JOHNNY MANDEL

CD
- **11** : SPLIT TRACK/MELODY
- **12** : FULL STEREO TRACK

♩: C VERSION

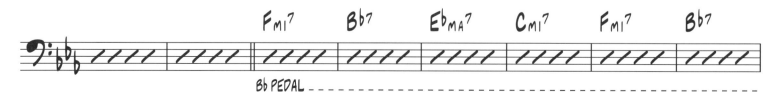

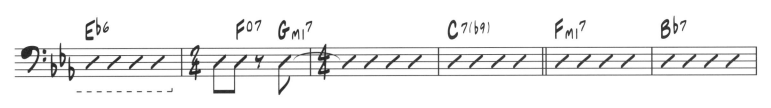

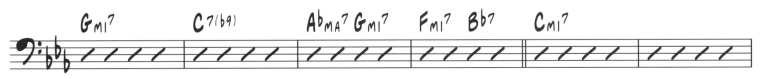

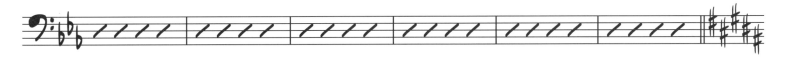

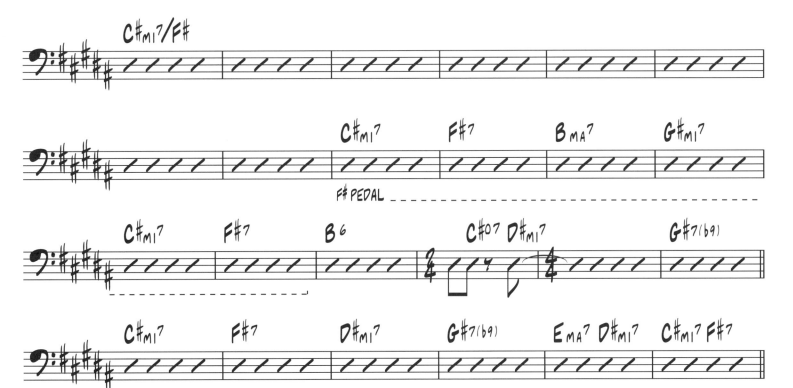

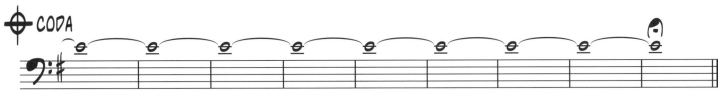

EMILY
FROM THE MGM MOTION PICTURE THE AMERICANIZATION OF EMILY

MUSIC BY JOHNNY MANDEL
WORDS BY JOHNNY MERCER

♭: C VERSION

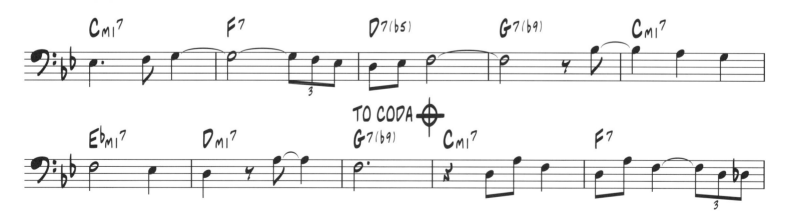

In Love in Vain

WORDS BY LEO ROBIN
MUSIC BY JEROME KERN

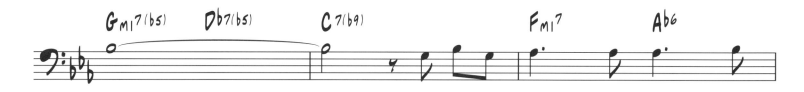

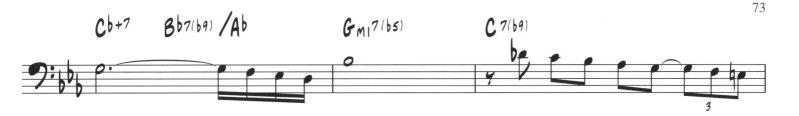

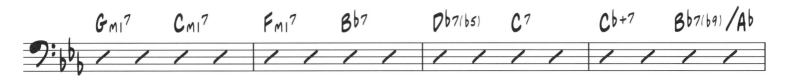
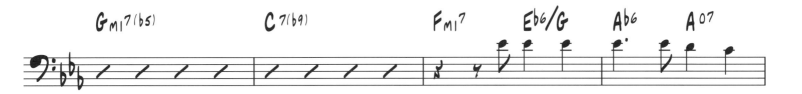

MY FOOLISH HEART
FROM MY FOOLISH HEART

WORDS BY NED WASHINGTON
MUSIC BY VICTOR YOUNG

RIT.

CD

7 : SPLIT TRACK/MELODY
8 : FULL STEREO TRACK

MY HEART STOOD STILL
FROM A CONNECTICUT YANKEE

WORDS BY LORENZ HART
MUSIC BY RICHARD RODGERS

🎼: C VERSION

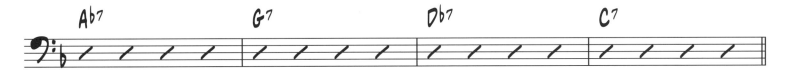

D.C. AL CODA
TAKE REPEAT

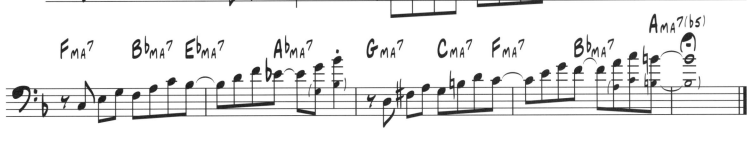

CD
- ◆ 9 : SPLIT TRACK/MELODY
- ◇ 10 : FULL STEREO TRACK

A SLEEPIN' BEE
FROM HOUSE OF FLOWERS

LYRIC BY TRUMAN CAPOTE AND HAROLD ARLEN
MUSIC BY HAROLD ARLEN

𝄢: C VERSION

Sweet and Lovely

WORDS AND MUSIC BY GUS ARNHEIM,
CHARLES N. DANIELS AND HARRY TOBIAS

C VERSION

81

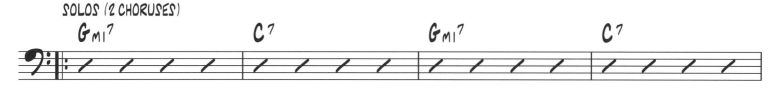

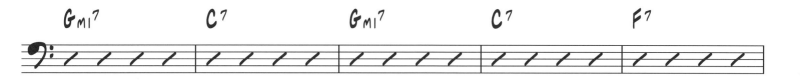

CD

15 : SPLIT TRACK/MELODY	
16 : FULL STEREO TRACK	

TENDERLY

FROM TORCH SONG

LYRIC BY JACK LAWRENCE
MUSIC BY WALTER GROSS

𝄢: C VERSION

MEDIUM WALTZ TEMPO

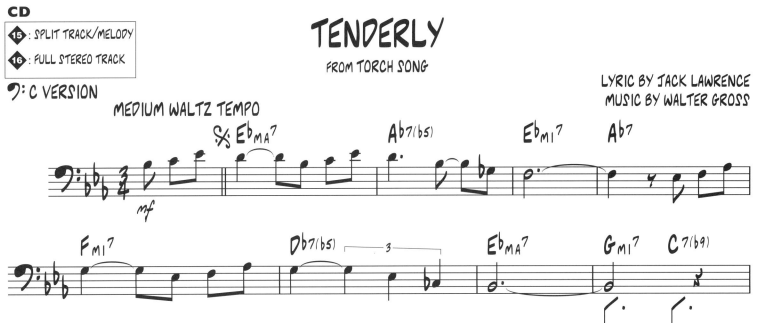

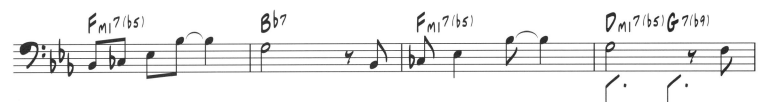

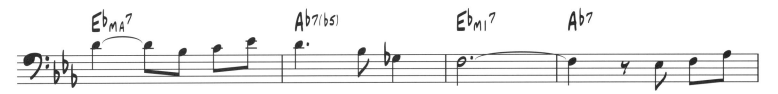

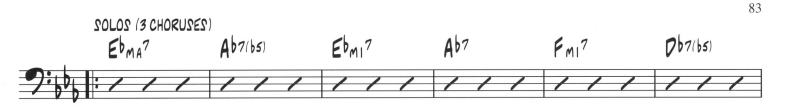

SOLOS (3 CHORUSES)

D.S. AL CODA

LAST X ONLY

CD

◆17 : SPLIT TRACK/MELODY
◆18 : FULL STEREO TRACK

𝄢: C VERSION

WHO CAN I TURN TO
(WHEN NOBODY NEEDS ME)

FROM THE ROAR OF THE GREASEPAINT – THE SMELL OF THE CROWD

WORDS AND MUSIC BY LESLIE BRICUSSE
AND ANTHONY NEWLEY

MEDIUM SWING

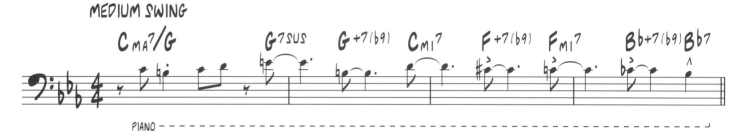

WITCHCRAFT

MUSIC BY CY COLEMAN
LYRICS BY CAROLYN LEIGH

𝄢: C VERSION

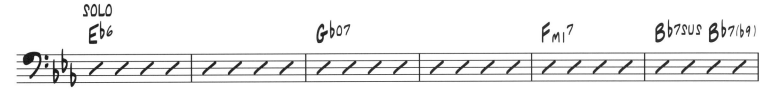

Presenting the Hal Leonard JAZZ PLAY-ALONG SERIES

For use with all B-flat, E-flat, Bass Clef and C instruments, the Jazz Play-Along® Series is the ultimate learning tool for all jazz musicians. With musician-friendly lead sheets, melody cues, and other split-track choices on the included CD, these first-of-a-kind packages help you master improvisation while playing some of the greatest tunes of all time. FOR STUDY, each tune includes a split track with: melody cue with proper style and inflection • professional rhythm tracks • choruses for soloing • removable bass part • removable piano part. FOR PERFORMANCE, each tune also has: an additional full stereo accompaniment track (no melody) • additional choruses for soloing.